For Catherine

THE IRISH PUB

PHOTOGRAPHY LIAM BLAKE

TEXT DAVID PRITCHARD

Published in Ireland by Real Ireland Design Limited

First published in 1997 by **Real Ireland Design Limited** ©.
27 Beechwood Close, Boghall Road, Bray, Co. Wicklow, Ireland.
Telephone: (01) 2860799. Fax: (01) 2829962.

Photography Liam Blake ©.
Text David Pritchard.
Book & jacket design Brian Murphy.

Printed in Ireland

British Library Cataloguing in Publication Data.
A catalogue record for this book is available from the British
Library

ISBN 0946887241

5 390946 887243

REAL IRELAND

INTRODUCTION

The Irish Pub is an unique institution, without any real equivalent elsewhere. Some may speak of Irish Christianity or literature as being the great contribution of our wet little island to the greater world beyond these shores. The true connoisseur of Irish culture knows, however, that these are pale shadows compared to the worldwide influence of our public houses and alcoholic beverages. To tens of millions of people around this globe who know what a Guinness is, Joyce remains only a girl's name and the Abbey Theatre might as well be the local movie house. Other nationalities perceive our pubs as an expression of the best elements of the Irish character, havens of wit, camaraderie and musical integrity. It is no accident that the pub's role in Ireland as the hub of communal and social existence, has been a feature of Irish life brought by emigrants to their new homes in America, Australia and Europe. The Irish expatriates who keep in contact with each other and events at home through their local Irish bars in Boston, Toronto, Brisbane and a hundred other cities, are following a hallowed tradition handed down by their forbears.

Despite its social and economic importance, the Public House has received remarkably little attention from historians and commentators. Liam Blake's photographs rectify this imbalance, offering a superb visual record of traditional Irish pubs from humble country bars to magnificent Victorian premises. His appreciation of the facades and decors of Irish pubs as forms of folk art is revealed by many of the images in this book. Other pictures explore more intangible aspects of the pub, its customers, atmosphere and contribution to Irish culture through music. As a whole, the images in this book constitute an invaluable photographic essay, celebrating a vital sector of the national heritage which has too often been ignored or trivialized.

The text which accompanies the pictures is divided into three parts. The first examines how pubs became so important in Irish life, and discusses their general development and architecture. The second draws on a representative selection of urban and rural pubs throughout Ireland which illustrate this history. The final part deals with the alcoholic drinks most associated with Ireland and the contribution of pubs to Irish culture through literature and music. It is our hope that the book will increase the reader's understanding and enjoyment of Ireland's traditional pubs and the people who drink in them.

HISTORY AND ARCHITECTURE

Ireland in the late twentieth century might be a land of rapidly accelerating change and sometimes destructive inno- vation, but one great national institution retains its integrity. The Irish Public House has survived into the computer age as the last arbiter of national and cultural values. Whilst the condom machine on its toilet wall may reflect a new acceptance of moral realities and personal choices repugnant to an older and more rigid generation, the pub's long established traditions of humour, good conversation and music remain as strong as ever.

Nobody would deny that the Irish pub is an unique institution, admired and imi- tated wherever emigrants from Ireland have settled. From New York to Sydney and beyond, 'Irish' bars sell stout and Irish whiskey to people whose ancestry

may be many generations removed from Ireland and yet who seek in them an affinity with a country they may never have seen. In recent decades the coming of mass tourism to Ireland and a new exodus of young Irish professionals has seen hundreds of 'Irish' bars opening in countries throughout Europe and even Asia, turning the Pub into a world wide phenomena. This is not an accidental event but a tribute to the worth of the Irish public house in a new media-driven World Culture which appreciates and yearns for its time honoured values.

Regardless of their international popu- larity, Irish Pubs began as an Irish response to local conditions and needs. For countless centuries the consumption of alcohol has been a major factor in the social life of this island and the pub plays an integral and very important role in the Irish scene. Which, of course, is not meant to imply that all Irish people are drunkards, or even drinkers. The temperance movement has been railing against the evils of the pub for almost a century and a half by now, and hundreds of thousands of Irish people have taken the 'pledge' and refrain from drinking intoxicating liquor of any kind. But even the pioneer must acknowledge that the little Sacred Heart badge in his collar is

The Brazen Head, Dublin's oldest pub.

a response - albeit a negative one - to the central position of alcohol in Irish cultural life. Whether you love it or loathe it the pub is at the hub of Irish life and to ignore its existence is tantamount to losing sight of the heart of the people.

The classic attitude of Irish drinkers to their local pub is encapsulated in the words of an old drinking song.
" Let's drink and be merry all griefs to refrain, for we may and might never all meet here again".
For many generations of Irish people driven by poverty to seek employment building the railways and cities of Britain and America the last line of the above quote has often been all too true. The drunken Irish labourer has long been a favourite stereotype in Britain and the U.S.A. and even Australia. Yet the reverse side to this figure is the tragic victim driven to alcoholism by forced exile from his homeland.

Notwithstanding their reputation at home and abroad, the Irish are by no means the heaviest drinkers in Europe and the problem of alcoholism - though bad enough - is no greater here than in a number of other countries. What marks Ireland out as unusual is the ambiguous national attitude towards heavy drinking. Traditionally a large capacity for alcohol has been considered an important masculine attribute and public drunkenness is tolerated to a far greater extent than elsewhere. 'In the part of Dublin I come from' said Brendan Behan, 'It is not considered a disgrace to get drunk, it is regarded as an achievement.' Whatever the reasons behind this attitude towards drinking - and they are no doubt complex - the Irish considered drinking a social occupation for the male only, something to be indulged in outside the home and away from the family. This is why the pub has been of such primary importance in the social life of the country, because as the gathering place of the male population it was where the important political issues of the day would be debated and a consensus of opinion arrived at. On this level the near total exclusion of the female has had a most harmful effect on the attitudes of men towards women in Ireland. It is a great relief to see that the pub has lost its misogynistic status as a male preserve in recent decades and now caters to both sexes equally. In coming to terms with such important issues as women's rights, the pint has been a more important catalyst to public opinion and attitude than the pulpit or the newspaper. For this rea-

O' Connells pub, Richmond Street, Dublin

son alone the role of the Pub in Irish life merits as serious consideration and discussion as that of the Church or Press.

Before going into details about this neglected part of the national heritage it is necessary to put forward some working definitions as to what constitutes a 'pub'. The Irish public house, the pub or bar as it is commonly called, is a premises licensed by the government to sell alcoholic beverages to the adult population. Irish licensing laws, which control the hours during which pubs are allowed to be open for business, are an adaptation of English laws, changed somewhat over the years to meet Irish conditions. There is still a false notion prevalent outside the country that all Irish pubs stay open both night and day, an attitude exemplified by the joke question 'When do the pubs around here close?' and its answer 'About September'. In reality the laws governing closing times are as strictly enforced by the police as possible, remembering of course that there are many pubs and not so many policemen. Though 'after hours' drinking goes on, the overwhelming majority of pubs operate within the legal time limit or face expensive court cases which might lead to the loss of their license.

Indeed, one of the staples of provincial newspapers is the prosecution of errant landlords and the heartbreaking excuses they produce for their pubs still having a dozen or so customers inside their doors at three o'clock in the morning.

Whilst pubs sometimes seem to have been part of the Irish scene for ever, they are in fact a comparatively recent introduction dating back mainly to the Victorian era. In its purest form the traditional pub grew out of the drinking dens of the people in earlier times and its sole function is to sell intoxicating liquors and provide a place to drink them. In practice, most pubs nowadays sell food and in rural areas might have a room or two to let for the night (if they have three bedrooms they probably call themselves a hotel). Over recent years Irish 'pub grub' has immensely improved and often offers exceptional quality and value for money, but the essence of a pub remains that it is a place where drinking takes precedence over all other activities.

The taverns of Medieval Europe, which catered to the needs of pilgrims and other travellers by providing food and accommodation as much as a place to meet and drink, were unknown in

Wall sign, Glendalough, Co. Wicklow.

Wall sign, Ballysadare, Co. Sligo.

Ireland, where the few roads were dangerous and outlaws made travel a hazardous occupation. There are no Irish equivalents, for example, to the ancient taverns along Pilgrims Road to St. Thomas Beckett's shrine at Canterbury in England, which so influenced the development of drinking establishments in that country. At a later stage Coaching Inns were opened on the more important Irish routes to serve coaches which delivered mail and passengers throughout the countryside. The best remaining example of these is the famous Brazen Head in Dublin, yet neither Coaching Inns nor the hotels in scenic areas which were built in the Victorian era to accommodate the tourist trade in Killarney and other beauty spots, were intended to be used by the bulk of the Catholic population.

The pub in its present form has its peculiarly Irish roots in the 19th. century,

Tom Long's bar, from Dingle Harbour.

when Dublin was the second city of the British Empire and brewing and distilling were becoming major Irish industries. The countryside was in the process of being opened up by canals and later the railway, and the products of Guinness and other manufacturers were finding new markets in remoter areas that they had hitherto been unable to reach. English was replacing Irish as the language of rural Ireland, and as part of the policy to make the country adhere more closely to English patterns there was a vigorous campaign against the illegal drinking place. This was notably helped along by the pioneer movement of Father Theobald Matthews in the 1840's, which resulted in the consumption of spirits being halved within a few short years. As the shebeen and the grog shop declined, they were replaced by licensed establishments where the emphasis was on beer and stout, rather than gin and whiskey. These 'public' houses rapidly established themselves as the common meeting place of the people and the

Cleary's bar, Amien Street, Dublin.

Private call in Dundalk pub.

Irish 'pub' was born.

The appearance and general milieu of the traditional Irish pub reflect its roots in the Victorian era. Unlike Britain, where public houses are generally owned by breweries, Irish pubs are privately owned, often over several generations by the same family. In most cases the pub will have either the owner's or the founder's name above it. This is far more common than the pub being given a name of its own, although there are exceptions where a pub's name refers to some local feature or event. Some newer pubs take their names from odd sources like popular movies, so it is possible to find oneself drinking in "The Graduate" or "The Godfather". However, Oliver St. John Gogarty once made the comment to the effect that whilst the name above the door might change, the pub will remain the same, and this remains true. When a new proprietor

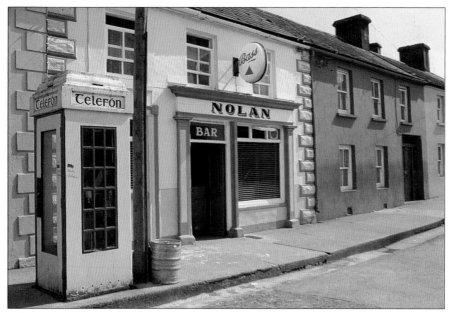

Nolan's pub, Union Hall, Co. Cork.

takes over a premises he is quite likely to change the name to his own without thinking of making any other alterations or renovations to the pub.

In size older pubs tend to be fairly small, ranging from the one room pub so common in rural areas to the larger and more ornate examples in the cities, which have a large bar plus a snug for the use of women and one or two private cubicles. Traditional pubs vary greatly in their appearance, depending on their environment and the tastes of their owners etc., but certain decorative motifs give them some uniformity of style. The traditional pub front is generally a late 19th. or early 20th. century development and must surely rate high as an example of local artistic endeavour and achievement. No two pub facades are exactly the same and they are often amongst the best decorated buildings in a town, adding greatly to the quality of street frontages.

Hanley's bar, Ballaghaderreen, Co. Roscommon.

Usually the pub will have its owner's name written on a board across the top of the windows, or in some smaller country pubs simply above the door. The hanging sign, although attractive, is an uncommon and modern feature probably copied from English pubs. In early pubs the owner's name was signpainted by hand above its window, but from the 1950's onwards it has been customary to use individual block letters, often gilded to give a more striking appearance. Many of the architectural features used in traditional fronts are classical in origin and it is common to see columns, cornices and fascia decorating the exteriors of older pubs. These are usually constructed of wood or plaster, often of exceptionally high quality workmanship, but in more opulent urban premises granite - and even marble - columns and facings are occasionally found. The very best pub exteriors are works of art, rich in marble, brass, glass and gold lettering and often executed in bold colours schemes. Utterly different, but equally fascinating in their own way, are the striking colours seen on the outside of some country pubs, or the primitive murals which occasionally enhance a whitewashed wall or gable end.

A particularly fetching aspect of both city and country pubs are the displays found in their windows, which often give an almost shoplike appearance. A standard feature are the whiskey and beer bottles placed there to entice the passer-by, but some landlords create quite artistic effects from bric-a-brac and curiosities. Model sail boats and curraghs are a common motif, as are carts, figurines and old pieces of pottery. A few establishments offer notably unusual and striking displays, for instance the Cartoon Inn in Rathdrum (Wicklow), which has an incongruous but magnificent wooden jazz band in its window.

Interior decor ranges from the extreme austerity of the small country pub at one end of the spectrum to the sumptuous Edwardian interiors of the finest Dublin and Belfast pubs at the other, but again certain features tend to be common to all. The pub mirror, advertising alcohol or tobacco, is found in most pubs and is generally an imposing piece of art in its own right. The counter of the pub is usually made of mahogany and holds taps through which draught beer is poured. Draught ales and stout are a comparatively recent innovation in many Irish pubs, and in most of them beer flows through little illuminated attachments provided by suppliers to advertise their beverages. But some older pubs still possess the earlier wooden pumps with brass attachments and these, when they are polished and shined, can be particularly attractive.

The pub clock, usually kept a few minutes fast to encourage customers to leave at closing time, takes a number of guises, the most typical perhaps being the round-faced mahogany version, which in some older pubs is built into the shelves behind the counter. A few pubs have 'American' pendulum clocks, so called because they were sent back by emigrants to the United States as presents. These clocks are recognisable by the name inscribed on them, which identifies the American city where they were made.

The area behind the counter, the 'bar', has had its name extended to give another term for the pub itself. The bar is the most brightly lit part of the premises, contrasting with the dim

Fox's pub and undertaker, Navan, Co. Meath.

recess where customers huddle over tables in deep and private conversations. In many older pubs gas lights preceded the electric light and a few establishments still possess their original brass lamps, now converted for electric bulbs. The Art-Nouveau stained glass Tiffany style light-shades in some pubs are generally recent introductions, which though of the appropriate period were probably uncommon in genuine Irish pubs of the Edwardian era.

The influence of Guinness, with its distinctive dark colour, is felt both inside and out. Probably all Irish pubs, old and new, have the Guinness sign on display in a variety of forms. The various advertising campaigns carried out by the company over the last century have had a strong effect on the 'look' of the Irish pub. Very commonly seen is the most famous of all Guinness slogans, 'GUINNESS IS GOOD FOR YOU', which

O' Donnabháin, Kenmare, Co. Kerry.

dates back to 1929 and has passed into the language as a catchphrase. The charming series of animal cartoons by James Gilroy are also seen here and there, and an unusual example has been included in the illustrations to this book. Sometimes the black and white motif is extended to include the whole exterior of the pub, as in the case of O'Donoghues of Merrion Row. Ultimately, given the importance of Guinness in Irish life, this is perhaps the most logical colour scheme of all for an Irish pub.

The rural pub has evolved along somewhat different lines to its counterparts in Dublin, Belfast and the other cities. By urban standards the peasant society of the Irish countryside might have been crude and impoverished, but within its still vigorous fabric were retained the remnants of an ancient Gaelic tradition of music and literature. The secular gathering place of the people was the shebeen, a primitive and illegal drinking den where poitín and other home made

Sign, Gormanston, Co. Meath.

Wall sign, Ballyvaughan, Co. Clare.

spirits were consumed in vast quantities. Here would come wandering performers, whose ancestors had been the bards and rhymers to the great Irish chieftains before the native aristocracy had been destroyed in the wars of the 16th. and 17th. centuries. In the shebeen there would be stories and recitations by Gaelic poets, and wild dancing to the fiddle and flute, played in a style whose origins went back to the remotest times. The itinerant musician and storyteller had an important role as the gatherer and dispenser of news. As he roved through the countryside he would keep the isolated clachan communities in touch with each other and with developments at home and abroad.

Rural Irish society, in religion Catholic and in language largely Gaelic speaking, was a closed book to the English who governed the country. Between the peasantry and the Protestant ruling class there was a relationship of innate hostility and an impenetrable wall of mistrust hid the inner life of the rural masses from their colonial landlords. The Irish peasant, excluded and isolated from power, responded externally to foreign domination with a blank stare or false smile. Behind this, however, his resentment and rage were funnelled into agrarian secret societies which fought an intermittent guerilla war against the cruellest landlords and their agents.

Some residue of this deep rooted secretiveness still permeates the atmosphere of the country pub. Hospitality to the stranger was one of the concepts at the heart of ancient Irish society and the visitor will meet few people as kind and generous as those he might encounter in a rural premises. Yet at the same time he will become aware of a curious shyness in those he speaks to when it comes to discussing local affairs, so unlike the Dublin pub - where a stranger will discuss his most private affairs without batting an eyelid. This reticence creates a boundary which the visitor cannot and should not try to penetrate. Whilst an outsider may catch a glimpse of the inner life of a rural community in its pub, only after a long residence in the area can he expect to be fully admitted into its society.

In modern times Irish society has been revitalised and the countryside is more alive than it has been for many generations. But the destruction to the rural psyche by the great famine of the 1840's was beyond measure, and it is undeniable that its residual effects may still be felt today. Whilst the immediate deaths by hunger were terrifying enough in themselves, greater damage was caused by the spectres of emigration and depopulation which emptied the countryside and sapped the will of the people. The late marriage became customary and the younger sons of farming families who did not emigrate usually remained unmarried so that land holdings could pass on undivided to the next generation. The once populous Irish countryside, before the Famine so alive and full of children, became a land of lonely middle-aged men and deserted farmsteads.

The masculine predominance in rural life has left a strong mark on the country pub. In pre-Famine times records indicate that women mingled freely with men in shebeens and grog houses. The intoxicated woman was a common enough sight and an old folk saying 'A drunken woman knows no shame' con-

Mulligan's pub & grocery, Stonybatter, Dublin.

demns such behaviour. However, in the late 19th. century a strongly moralistic tendency in the Catholic Church imposed strict new standards of behaviour on the Irish people. The very idea of men and women drinking together came to be considered improper and even indecent. The pub became a male preserve, into which women were not allowed to enter. This attitude lasted well into modern times, and there are still probably many pubs with bars where women are frowned on.

In earlier pubs the near total exclusion of females is reflected in the 'snug', a partitioned off area near the front door, where women were tolerated provided they did not enter the main body of the public house. In Dublin and Belfast, where the influence of the church was never quite as strong as elsewhere, this unspoken rule was not always adhered to. In the male orientated bachelor society of rural Ireland, however, women were more vulnerable to social condem-

Doheny & Nesbitt, Baggot Street, Dublin.

nation. The male dominance of the pub became absolute and older premises made no provisions for women customers. Until the last decade or so, it was possible to walk into a pub on some remote Atlantic peninsula and find oneself sharing the bar with a couple of dozen men, mostly middle aged and all wearing their overcoats, with not a woman in sight.

The true country pub, as befits its descent from the shebeen, tends to be smaller and more Spartan in its fittings than its cousins in Dublin and the smaller towns. Ellen's Pub, a little thatched bar in a remote part of Co. Sligo, offers some idea of the appearance of shebeens, and with its fine local musicians hints at the uninhibited atmosphere of earlier times. The older, unrenovated, country pub will as often as not, consist of no more than a small room with a mahogany counter and a few wooden tables and chairs. Decorations will be minimal, quite possibly comprising no

Fitzgerald's bar, Avoca, Co. Wicklow.

more than a few inconsequential pieces of bric-a-brac and an old calendar or print on the wall. The austerity of these rural public houses has led to suggestions that they indicate inbred feelings of guilt on the part of the Irishman about his drinking habits, a belief that drinking was less of a sin if carried out in uncongenial surroundings. This seems overly fanciful, it being more likely that economic conditions were so bad that publicans could not afford to spend money on decorating their premises and making

them more comfortable.

Rural pubs are scattered around the countryside quite profusely wherever there are people, even in some remote areas. The classic country premises is perhaps the crossroads pub, grocery and (sometimes) Post Office, which at one time was distributed every two or three miles along main roads in farming districts. These establishments usually date from the early decades of this century and are often not much larger than

Wall sign near Ballinrobe, Co. Mayo.

Pub door, Brandon, Co. Kerry.

a medium sized two-storey farmhouse. Typically the grocery part of the premises will be on one side of the ground floor, with a partitioned-off bar on the other and living quarters upstairs. They were built when cars were still uncommon and rural transport was mainly by cart or foot. Crossroad pubs provided a shop and meeting place for people in the immediate locality, and for this reason were commonly sited at important crossroads some miles away from the nearest town. Today most farming families have cars or tractors and sadly these pub/groceries have become redundant and are in decline.

Pubs with dual function were once equally common both in cities and small market towns, the most extraordinary, perhaps, being those that also served as local undertakers. Whether in town or city, it was not uncommon for such dual purpose businesses to take a corner site,

Dick Mack's pub, Dingle, Co. Kerry.

P Mac Namara's pub, Bunratty folkvillage, Co. Clare.

with the pub facing onto one street and the grocery or hardware store onto the other. The urban pub/shop is a great rarity now and the few remaining examples are unlikely to survive in the era of the supermarket and the shopping centre.

A remarkable feature of many small towns is the large number of pubs to be seen, and it is not uncommon to find three or four licensed premises in a row along a street. These drinking places exist to serve the inhabitants of the surrounding areas as well as townsfolk. The pubs are especially busy on market days, when local farmers come to town for supplies and to buy and sell cattle and other livestock. In addition to their traditional role as a place for a quiet drink after the day's work, at these times country pubs become an impromptu office, where traders and dealers can complete their bargains with a handshake and thirst quenching pint of stout. Gossip and information are exchanged with the cattle dealers and other merchants visiting the fair from outside the region. Even in this age of television and daily newspapers, pubs in country towns still retain some of their role as windows on the outside world.

The old pubs of Dublin, Belfast and other cities have a very different quality to rural pubs. Most of Dublin's famous licensed premises date from the Victorian era, when she was becoming a large city, a little seedy, perhaps, in comparison to the days of her Georgian glory, but with a large population (including an English garrison) who needed places to mingle and drink. Notwithstanding her ghastly slums and red-light district, Dublin was a relaxed and friendly city for the most part, where the various sections of the population mixed freely within the doors of her pubs and hotel bars. In this cosmopolitan city, with its witty and eloquent proletariat, the pub developed into a neutral ground where class distinctions could be dropped and good conversation indulged as an end in itself. Tom Corkery wrote about this tradition as he saw it continued on into the late 1950's.

'Yet the poet could and did share the same pub with the peasant and no man had need of looking up, down or askance at his fellow man. Patrick Kavanagh could be heard discoursing in McDaid's of Harry Street on such esoteric subjects as professional boxing, the beauty of Ginger Rogers, or the dire state of Gaelic Football in Ulster. Flann O'Brien could be heard in Neary's or in the Scotch House

The Mill's Inn, Ballyvourney, Co. Cork.

on any subject known to man. Brendan Behan could be seen and heard everywhere.'
From: 'Tom Corkery's Dublin (Anvil Books)'

The Dublin Pub of today may retain its Victorian roots, but is is likely to have been restored in the 1960's and 1970's. Alternatively it can be a new premises in pseudo pub-Victorian, an unique and generally ghastly decorative style which seems to have evolved specifically for the furbishing of Irish public houses. In the capital, and indeed the other cities, the street-scape has been evolving for many decades. The expansion of suburbs over the last forty years has led to the founding of many new pubs and the restoration of older establishments. Whilst these larger pubs, which have usually added a mixed Lounge to the older 'Men-only' bar and Snug, are more comfortable in their surroundings and sometimes retain interesting facades, they lack the charac-

The Greyhound pub, Kinsale, Co. Cork.

ter of the old-style premises, which are sadly becoming rarer as the years go by. The traditional pub, whether in town or country, has an intrinsic artistic and cultural value of its own which makes it as important a part of the nation's architectural heritage as other historical buildings. The owners and landlords of older public houses, when planning changes to their premises, have a duty to give this legacy equal consideration to their commercial needs.

THE PUBS OF IRELAND

According to the best estimates there are over 11,000 pubs in Ireland. What constitutes a good pub is a matter of taste or personal interest of course and one man's convivial home from home can be another's smokey, boring hell. Different people find pleasures in their pubs and this is the way it should be. Also pubs change; last year's nicotine middle-aged man's spit and sawdust local can be this year's neon and plastic karaoke teenagers' disco. Nevertheless there are certain pubs which because of their historical connections, traditional decor or sheer atmosphere stand out above the rest. To pick out some of these as 'notable' is not an attempt to denigrate thousands of other exceptional pubs, each with their own stories and distinguishing features. Rather a selection of premises must stand as a cross section for all the fine and interesting pubs of Ireland.

To start perhaps, the few genuinely ancient pubs in Ireland should be mentioned. Taverns were undoubtedly found in medieval Irish towns, but like most vernacular buildings dating from before 1700, their premises have almost totally disappeared. The most famous of the few Irish pubs with medieval connections is Kyteler's Inn in Kilkenny. The ground floor of the pub is a tastefully restored bar and restaurant, but its cellar was probably built in the 14th. or 15th. century and overlooks the ancient holy well of St. Kieran. The building was once the home of Alice Kyteler, the protagonist in the most famous witchcraft trial in Irish history. In 1324, she was accused of worshipping the devil and sentenced to be executed. Following the trial, which may have been motivated by her political enemies, Dame Alice escaped to England but her unfortunate maid Petronilla was burnt at the stake.

Another pub in an ancient building may be found in Shop Street, Galway. Whilst 'The Snug' is not itself particularly old, its premises are in a stone cellar which probably dates back to at least the 16th. century. An alcove in the back of the pub is situated in the hearth of the original medieval chimney. The Abbey Tavern in Howth, a few miles north of Dublin, started to do business in 1740. It gains its name from the ancient abbey against which it was built and parts of the tavern incorporate stonework from the 1400's. The 'Abbey' is one of the best known pubs, restaurants and entertainment venues in north Dublin.

A number of Northern Irish pubs are exceptionally old. The Crawfordsburn Inn (Co. Down), a moderately sized hotel south of Belfast Lough, has a history going back to the end of the 16th. century. It received the first rave revue of any Irish pub in 1603, when an English traveller praised its food and wine in his diary. The thatched inn has many superb features, not least its magnificent stone fireplace and a fine 17th. century chandelier. Another Down pub, Grace

Interior of Ryan's pub, Parkgate Street, Dublin.

O' Sullivan's bar, Ballydehob, Co. Cork.

O'Neill's of Donaghadee, can claim to be amongst Ireland's oldest pubs, with a history dating back to 1611, although Grace O'Neill herself lived in the 19th. century. In the Republic the oldest pub is probably at the Woodenbridge Hotel (Wicklow), which started as a coach stop on the important Wexford route just after 1600.

Whilst there are a number of other pubs which can claim descent from early taverns, the majority of surviving pre-19th.

century drinking establishments were originally situated in Inns designed to service coach routes. The golden age of Coaching Inn was in the 1700's, when the countryside was being developed by Anglo-Irish landlords and new market towns were coming into existence throughout rural Ireland. The Brazen Head, the oldest pub in Dublin, was chartered in 1688 and its present building, complete with a courtyard for coaches and horses, erected in 1700. The inn is very unlike a Victorian or modern

Crown bar (detail), Belfast.

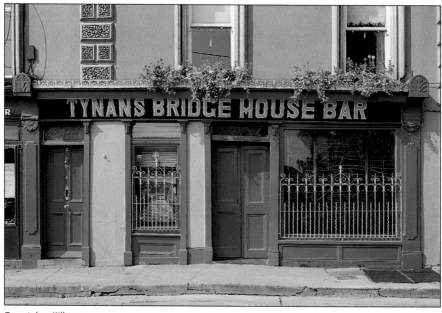

Tynan's bar, Kilkenny.

premises, having a number of smallish rooms and nooks and crannies rather than a large open bar or lounge. It has strong (and genuine) connections to the leaders of the United Irishmen - who used it for meetings - and Robert Emmet, who stayed at the Inn whilst plotting the 1803 Rising. Another fine Coaching Inn is the Roundwood Inn in Roundwood (Wicklow). Like a number of other Co. Wicklow pubs, for instance the Wicklow Arms in Delgany, it is noted for its exceptional 'pub grub', which brings customers to the premises from as far away as the suburbs of Dublin.

The natural successors to Coaching Inns were railway hotels like the Great Southern in Galway (built in 1845) and the tourist hotels, which from the beginning of the Victorian era onwards were built to accomodate the English visitors and commercial travellers already touring Ireland in large numbers. Where they survive in original form, the public areas of Victorian hotels have a sedate

The Marble City bar, Kilkenny.

and gentle ambience very different to that of the typical pub. Even today the bars of older quality Irish hotels like the Shelbourne (Dublin) have a noticeably more class conscious and exclusive atmosphere than the everyday pub.

If there were a world centre for pubs it would be Dublin, which has well over a thousand. These range in size from small and simple working class pubs to the huge modern mega-premises with bars, lounges, discos and restaurants.

Choosing a representative sample is a particularly difficult task because of the sheer number and quality of the capital's pubs. A good starting point might be John Mulligan's of Poolbeg Street, in many ways the quintessential Dublin pub. The pub is quite old by Irish standards, having first received its license in 1782. As it stands it is mainly a production of the Victorian and Edwardian eras, with a fine wooden exterior and an interior with three unspoiled bars and a large upstairs lounge. The pub started

Herrity's bar, Co. Donegal.

Mc Hugh's bar, Ardara, Co. Donegal.

life as a local for the workers of the area, but became a favourite with other groups. In earlier days, when the old Theatre Royal was across the street, it was frequented by actors and a Music Hall crowd, hence the old theatrical posters on its wall. The merchants of the old Corn Exchange, now demolished, made use of the 'posher' upstairs area of the pub at lunchtime and after work. Finally, journalists from the newspaper offices in the vicinity (including many

who are now world famed writers) would congregate in the nooks and crannies of Mulligan's to share some of the wittiest conversations ever heard in an Irish pub.

Many of Dublin's finest pubs are late Victorian in origin, undoubtedly the era when pub architecture and decor were at their best. Ryan's of Parkgate Street is amongst the finest unspoiled Victorian premises of the era, with a magnificent carved mahogany bar, brass beer pumps,

Hennessy's bar, Ferbane, Co. Offaly.

snug and all the trappings of a pub of the 1890's. It is rivalled by one of its near contemporaries, the Stag's Head in Dame's Court, opened in 1890.
The building which houses this pub is a fine example of the red brick architecture which was popular in Victorian times, whilst its red Connemara marble bar counter is a superb specimen of a type often seen in the best furnished Irish pubs of the age. The carved and decorated partitions which divide up the length of the counter were another com-

mon feature, intended to give drinkers at the bar a little privacy.

Kavanagh's, in the suburb of Glasnevin, is a little less ornate, but has perhaps the best preserved interior of any 'traditional' Dublin pub. The premises is situated beside Prospect cemetery and legend has it that in former times the gravediggers would stick their shovels through a hole provided in the wall for a pint to refresh them as they worked. Doheny and Nesbitt's of Baggot Street

Row of pubs, Ennistymon, Co. Clare.

ranks with Kavanagh's as an above average example of the old style pub, although it started its commercial existence as a tea and wine merchant. The pub is surprisingly large behind its traditional shop frontage. The mirrored frame in the front window advertising whiskey and other drinks was a popular method of screening off the interior of pubs from passers by, whilst a long brass plaque beneath the window serves as a reminder of the premises previous business. Its situation in the midst of one of

the city's most important business districts has made Doheny and Nesbitts into one of the busiest and most cosmopolitan pubs in Ireland, usually packed out even on week nights.

Not too far away is O'Donoghues, with its familiar black and white facade. This equally busy pub has a claim to be the most famous in Dublin due to its association with the Dubliners' folk group. The late Luke Kelly, perhaps the archetypal singer and poet of the Irish working

Cooley's bar, Ennistymon, Co. Clare.

classes, was a regular here and the walls of the back room are covered with photographs of other great musicians who have played in the pub. O'Donoghue's continues to be one of the best known music pubs in Dublin, sometimes with several sessions going on simultaneously. An even busier music pub is Slattery's of Capel Street, originally a mid Victorian pub/grocery shop but now one of the most important small music venues in the city, with two lounges featuring live performers. Many of the best known Irish traditional and rock musicians played in Slattery's in their formative years and the pub still provides an important platform for minority tastes like Blues, Jazz and Country music.

The Bailey on Duke Street, now one of the most fashionable Dublin pubs, has connections with many of the great Irish political and literary figures of the last century. According to tradition the upper room was used by Parnell and the Irish Party in the 1880's and was also a

Mc Daid's, Dublin city.

O' Donaghue's pub, Merrion Row, Dublin.

favourite meeting place of the Invincibles, the revolutionary group who committed the Phoenix Park murders in 1882. In the early part of this century the 'Bailey' group, centered around Arthur Griffith, the first president of Ireland, included writers like Padraic Colum, Oliver St. John Gogarty and James Stephens. Around the 1960's the Bailey experienced something of a literary renaissance with a new generation of writers like Ulick O'Connor and J.P. Donleavy. McDaid's of Harry Street, with

its brightly painted facade, is perhaps Dublin's other most important 'literary' pub. In the 1940's and 50's it was the local of Brendan Behan, whilst the poet Patrick Kavanagh, the novelist Flan O'Brien and a number of other lesser known writers were regular visitors.

Davy Byrne's of Duke Street, James Joyce's 'Moral Pub' of Ulysses, has undergone major changes since 1940 but remains a popular and interesting premises, although somewhat mod-

Griffin's bar, Ennistymon, Co. Clare.

ernised. Toner's of Baggot Street, a delightful traditional pub dating back to the 1830's, has perhaps the oddest literary connection of all the pubs of Dublin. It claims to be the only pub ever visited by W.B.Yeats. According to the story he was brought here for a drink at the insistence of Oliver St. John Gogarty. The poet drank a sherry in the snug, then turned to Gogarty and said 'I've seen a pub. Now would you kindly take me home' and stalked out without another word.

In today's Dublin, a cosmopolitan city with a large population, the Victorian pub competes with newer premises - many in a pseudo-traditional style that might be called 'Art Alcho' - and imaginative ultra modern bars like those at the Clarence Hotel (Wellington Quay) and the Irish Film Centre (Eustace Street). This mixture is not unhealthy and the city's pub scene is as vibrant as ever, with a remarkable choice of good drinking establishments. Despite the

Con Macken's bar and undertakers, Wexford town.

emergence of Licensed Restaurants and Wine Bars, the Dublin pub is as thriving an institution as it ever was.

The pubs of Ireland's other cities reflect the cultures and attitudes of their own inhabitants as much as those of Dublin. Belfast's are influenced by its expansion during the 19th. century from a small country town into a great Victorian industrial city. Kelly's Cellars in Bank Lane is probably's Belfast's oldest premises, with a history that goes back to 1720. In the 1780's it was frequented by Henry Joy McCracken, the heroic leader of the Ulster United Irishmen, who once hid beneath the counter to avoid arrest by English soldiers. The downstairs area of the pub, which has many other associations with famous citizens of Belfast, harks back to the days before the city's growth, when Kelly's was a simple country tavern.

The queen of Belfast's pubs is undoubtedly the Crown Liquor Saloon in Great

Davy Byrne's pub, Dublin.

Healy's bar, Wicklow town.

Dan Foley's pub, Annascaul, Co. Kerry.

Victoria Street. The pub was first established in 1826 but owes its present spectacular appearance to the work of Italian craftsmen who refurbished the premises in 1885. In the magnificence of its facades and interior this superb pub is untypical of Ireland, being related rather to large premises in northern English cities like Manchester. Architecturally it is an extraordinary example of high Victorian decorative tastes, with mosaic-, tile- and wood-work equal to that of major 19th. century churches like Westminster Cathedral. The Crown has no less than ten snugs off its downstairs bar, plus an upstairs lounge partly built with the timbers of the Brittanic, the sister ship of the doomed Titanic.

The Crown Liquor Saloon is owned and preserved by the National Trust, who lovingly restored it to its original appearance in the early 1980's. Two smaller Victorian pubs which deserve a mention are the Kitchen Bar (Victoria Square), once a local for performers at the old Empire Music Hall, and the Morning Star (Pottinger's Entry), situated in a listed early 19th. century premises. Often, however, many of the pubs in Belfast's city centre are new buildings or modern restorations in revivalist pub styles. Two of the Crown's near neighbours illustrate this tendency at its most spectacular.

The Beaten Docket was built in 1985 and has a glass dome which is illuminated at night. The ground floor is designed to imitate the typical Victorian style, with long mohogany, counter etc., whilst the upstairs area is more modern, with strong hints of Art Deco in many of its details and furnishings. Robinson's, on the other hand, was a well respected Victorian pub until destroyed by an I.R.A. bomb some years ago. Its owners restored part of the original pub in a traditional style, using material salvaged from the old pub where possible. The rest of the building was converted into a complex of 'theme' bars, with four floors ranging from a 'speakeasy' to a 'bikers' bar in the basement.

Pubs like the Beaten Docket and Robinson's have come a long way from the old style working man's pub. They represent an attitude towards drinking very different to that of our forbears, who took their alcohol more seriously and without the sense of fun one sees in the young people crowding the bars of Ireland's cities today. Yet on another level the designer pub is an heir to the opulence of the Crown Liquor Saloon, where the exuberance of the premises

Egan's pub, Moate, Co. Meath.

has become part of the experience of going for a drink. As much as the other activities that go on behind their doors, pub decors now offer entertainment and seek to dictate the tone of the clientele.

The pubs of Cork, as in many other things, are a law unto themselves. Murphy's and Beamish, the city's local stouts, rival Guinness in the local pubs, which include a number of exceptional premises. The Long Valley (Winthrop Street), opened in 1842, is one of Cork's most important pubs, with notably good old wooden interior furbishments and details. The Oyster Tavern (Market Lane) is even older, having been established in the late 18th. century. Like many Cork pubs it was originally owned by one of the numerous brewers who were active in the city during the 18th. and 19th. centuries. Another 200 year old pub, although it has been totally rebuilt, is the Vineyard, one of the most popular meeting places in the city.

McDonagh's bar, Oranmore, Co. Galway.

The other Irish cities have fine traditional pubs of their own. In Galway, Naughton's (Tigh Neachtain) of Cross Street has an interior unchanged since it was opened in 1894. The pub is situated in a fine old town house which has much medieval work in its fabric. O'Connell's of Eyre Square was a grocery/pub until about 25 years ago, but retains most of its original decor. Sligo's finest old pub is Hargadon's (O'Connell Street), an almost pristine example of a middling sized country pub of the early 20th. century. There are four small snugs and the shelves of its old grocery section are still intact. Limerick's many traditional pubs include Tom Collin's (Cecil Street) and South's (O'Connell Street), which can boast a particularly impressive bar area with a partitioned white marble counter.

Kilkenny, a brewing town where the local ale, Smithwick's, has been brewed since 1710, is fortunate to possess two of the finest old pubs in Ireland. The Marble City Bar (High Street) is a gem of a small traditional premises, with a simple but striking red frontage with gold lettering. The equally distinctive blue facade of Tynan's Bridge House will be familiar to anybody driving into the city from the direction of Dublin. This exceptional premises was once a grocery and pharmacy as well, hence the lovely wooden drawers behind the bar for foodstuffs and the scale standing on its counter. Many rank Tynan's amongst the best traditional pub interiors in Ireland.

With the exception of those pubs that started life as Coaching Inns, country pubs are usually very basic and quite shop-like, often with small windows rather than the plate glass fronts of most urban pubs. The most prized are probably thatched pubs, but these are quite uncommon, since slates and tiles have generally replaced thatch over the last century. Whilst a number of small shop-style pubs with thatched roofs, like M.O'Shea of Faugheen (Kilkenny) and Hennessy's of Ferbane (Offaly), may still be seen around the country, premises in traditional style cottages are rarer. Ellen's Pub in Maugherow (Sligo) is a rare example of a pub situated in a thatched longhouse dwelling. There appears to have been a dwelling on the site for over 300 years, but the porch and windows of the present building are comparatively modern.

The small rural pub still thrives in a few parts of the country. Amongst the best known is M.J. Byrne's in Greenan, Co. Wicklow, a few miles from the spectacular valley of Glenmalure. This tiny premises, adjacent to a crenellated carriage entrance, is remarkably well known outside of its catchment area, thanks mainly to the hill walkers and holiday makers who throng the Wicklow hills every summer. Like the Glenmalure Lodge, a few miles further down the road, it often attracts traditional musicians for sessions at night. A third premises in the area, Phelan's of Ballinaclash, remains a genuine pub/grocers catering to the locals in its small community and the surrounding farming district.

At the time of writing the most famous Irish publican is John B. Keane of Listowel (Kerry), whose plays about rural life are the modern heirs to the works of Synge and the other Abbey playwrights. His literary success is not at odds with his profession, since rural landlords are often remarkable for their wit and surprisingly wide interests. Commonly they are amongst the leaders in their small

O' Sullivan's pub, Allihies, West Cork.

Murphy's pump, Healy Pass, Co. Kerry.

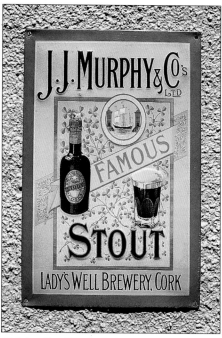

Wall sign, Clonakilty, Co. Cork.

communities and the guardians of local folk memory and custom. The late Dan Foley, whose colourful pub in Annascaul (Kerry) is one of the most photographed in Ireland, may serve as an example of the breed. A farmer by trade, he was at the same time an imaginative and forward looking publican and an expert on the history of the Kerry area. He also contrived to be a fine conversationalist and was reputedly an eager amateur magician. Like innumerable other good

landlords in country towns, his endeavours helped revive the local economy by bringing in extra tourism and trade to the area.

One of the more remarkable aspects of pubs in country areas and small towns is how just small they are in many cases. Several pubs lay claim to be the smallest in Ireland, but the best contender is probably Mary McBride's, a one room 'parlour' premises in Cushendun

(Antrim). This tiny bar, which is owned by the National Trust, is named after its almost legendary owner, a teetotaller who refused to serve women in her pub. Yet although Mary McBride's is remarkably diminutive, many a pub in the countryside and villages of Ireland is not that much bigger.

Take as an example, the pubs of the little towns around the Burren of Clare. Ennistymon has an extraordinary number of small bars, and they are by far the most numerous commercial premises in the place. This goes back to the days when pubs were also grocers or other merchants and drink was an additional service provided for customers. Settlements like Ennistymon, Corrofin and Lahinch might seem like hotbeds of alcoholism if their pubs are counted by the outsider. In reality they were just towns where the local shop would provide a drink after the groceries were bought. With the opening of newsagents and supermarkets in most country towns, these small groceries lost their customers, encouraging owners to concentrate on their alcohol business. The rise in car ownership (which makes it easier for surrounding farmers to come to town) and tourism helps these small pubs survive in a changing commercial environment. The few remaining dual purpose pubs, such as Dick Mack's of Dingle - which is also a leather goods shop - often survive today partly because of their novelty value.

The small pubs of western counties like Clare, Kerry and Sligo, played a notable role in preserving traditional Irish music and have now become its window to the world. At one level the laws introduced in the 18th. and 19th. centuries to control drinking, brewing and distilling, might be seen as part of an overall policy to replace Irish culture with English standards. The success of these attempts is indicated by the disappearance of the Irish language and the abandonment of the traditional cottage for small farmhouses and bungalows. The survival of traditional music through long years of neglect is in part a tribute to the country pub as a retainer and transmitter of the values and heritage of traditional Ireland. In this context pubs like O'Connor's of Doolin or Hennessy's of Milltown Malbay, which nurtured great Clare musicians like the piper Willy Clancy, are especially deserving of mention.

Today, so many rural pubs encourage good Irish music that it is necessary to

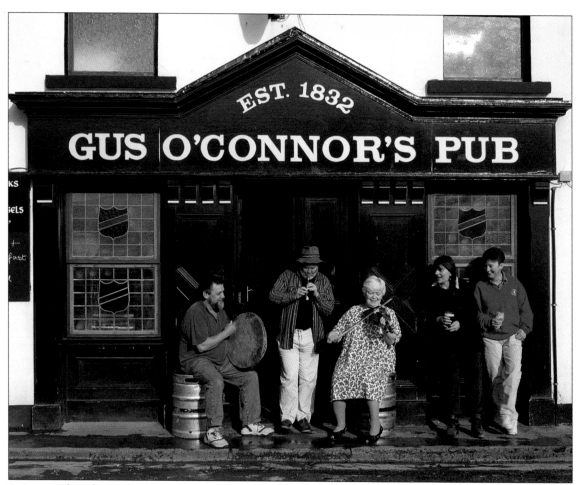

O' Connor's pub, Doolin, Co. Clare.

Pub music session, Milltown Malbay, Co. Clare.

mention only one or two. O'Flaherty's of Dingle is amongst the best known music pubs in Kerry, whilst in Connaught Matt Molloy's of Westport (Mayo) offers some of the best authentic Irish music. Donegal and Ulster have a particularly strong musical heritage, which greatly influenced the development of early American folk styles. The tradition is still vibrant, as may be seen in Croskey's Inn, Port Glenone (Antrim), an old thatched pub which features Ulster players and singers.

The revival of interest in Irish music has brought many young people to seek out the authentic sources of the style, helping to bring a new lease of life to a dying tradition. Irish music has been rescued from the anthropologist and the Folklore Archive and returned to the people, a development in which the Irish pub has taken a major role. There is nothing more heartening than seeing an old traditional musician in some small bar passing his skills to a young - and quite often foreign - enthusiast. If good con-

Gartland's thatched pub, Kingscourt, Co. Cavan.

versation and a ready wit are the great contribution of the pubs of Dublin, Belfast and Cork to the Irish psyche, the country pubs have passed on a musical legacy which helps define the shared culture of the whole island.

DRINK, MUSIC AND LITERATURE.

Since its inception the Irish pub has always reflected the greater society of which it is such an integral part. The economic importance of the alcohol industry in Ireland, which provides Irish people with thousands of jobs, is one aspect of its influence. The literary and musical legacies of the pub are cultural counterparts of its commercial contribution, and in their own way of equal significance. Decor and architecture are

O' Flaherty's bar, Dingle, Co. Kerry.

Wall sign, Co. Antrim.

only part of the 'pub experience' and to fully understand its Irishness we must investigate these other factors.

The nature of the Irish pub has been very much determined by the development of the Irish alcohol industry. Without doubt the types of drink which are consumed in Ireland have had a powerful influence on the habits of the people. 'Whiskey would make a rabbit spit at a dog' according to an old Gaelic proverb describing the fiery spirit which is per-

haps the most uniquely Irish drink of all. It was first distilled in Ireland well over a thousand years age, probably by monks who had come in contact with spirit making on missionary journeys through Europe. Alternatively it might have been developed here by Benedictine monks, who are believed to have set up abbeys in Ireland during the 8th. century. Unlike their counterparts on the continent, who used wine as a base, the Irish made their distillation from barley and thus invented the spirit called 'uisce beatha' or the

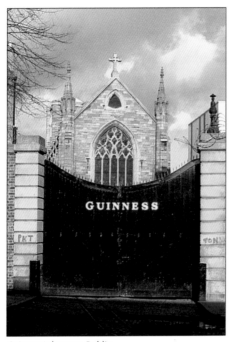

Guinness's brewery, Dublin.

Mac Carthy's bar, Castletownbere, Co. Cork.

'water of life' in tribute to its medical qualities.

Whiskey became the staple alcoholic beverage of the Irish countryside and remained so right up to the end of the 19th. century. No doubt its fiery qualities had much to do with the legendary wildness of Irish fairs, where vast quantities of whiskey were consumed. Whiskey drinking also contributed to the murderous savagery of the notorious faction fights which were such a notable feature of the period and contributed strongly to the reputation of the Irish as violent and pugnacious drinkers.

Pot stilled Irish whiskey is distinguished from 'Scotch', its blended Scottish counterpart (spelt without the e), by being distilled three times after fermentation rather than twice as in Scotland.

A couple of centuries ago there were

In Smith's bar, Dunlaoghaire, Dublin.

D. O' Shea's, Sneem, Co. Kerry.

over a thousand licensed distilleries operating in Ireland, as well as countless illegal stills producing poitin, an unsanctioned spirit usually made on a potato base (though often barley would be used to distil a crude whiskey). Since then more rigorous government control, changing drinking habits and the setting up of large distilleries have reduced this number radically. Nowadays one very large amalgamated company, the Irish Distilleries Group (set up in 1966), controls the distribution of most of the whiskeys and other spirits made in Ireland.

It is under their trademark you will find the great brands of Irish Whiskies that are so much a part of the Irish pub tradition. The best known Irish whiskeys are probably Powers, Paddy and Jameson. In more sectarian times it was claimed that you could tell a whiskey drinker's religion by his chosen brand, the Catholics going

De Barra's Bar, Clonakilty, Co. Cork.

for Powers whilst the Protestants preferred Jameson. The oldest of the surviving distilleries is situated up near the Giant's Causeway in County Antrim and has been making whiskey continuously since 1609. Its product, the Old Bushmills brand, is particularly noteworthy in flavour. Whiskey, drunk straight down or as a chaser to a pint of stout, has always, by custom, been the classic man's drink in Irish pubs. These are changing times and many new and varied drinks are being sampled in Ireland's

bars and lounges. Still, the combination of Irish whiskey and stout remains both popular and powerful and is probably the most representative example of the traditional tastes of Ireland's drinkers.

There are of course, other fine Irish spirits and liquers. Gin has a long history in Ireland, most notably as the favourite of urban women, whilst more recent introductions like Vodka and Rum are popular with the younger generation. Irish whiskey liqueurs, particularly those like

Whiskey mirror, Dingle, Co. Kerry.

Wall sign, on the Ring of Kerry.

Baileys which use cream, have become extremely successful in recent years and provide a sizable income to the National economy from export sales. Over the last decade wine based drinks and even natural spring waters like Ballygowan have become very fashionable in Irish pubs, perhaps partly in response to stricter drink driving laws. Yet the spirit from barley - whether drunk straight, hot with cloves or in the ubiquitous 'Irish Coffee' - retains its unique place in the hearts of the Irish drinker.

The name Guinness has become identified with Ireland all over the world. The most important date in the history of Irish brewing is undoubtedly December 1, 1759, on which date Arthur Guinness opened his brewery at St. James's Gate on the banks of the River Liffey. From this small premises has grown the great industrial empire that is so entwined in Irish life and culture. Today the Guinness empire sells its products in over one hundred and fifty countries to peoples as diverse as the Japanese, Canadians and Nigerians.

The porters and stouts for which Guinness are famous were not originally a native Irish brew. Barley beer is one of the oldest alcoholic beverages known to man, dating back to the earliest farming communities of ten thousand years ago. It was almost certainly known in prehistoric Ireland, but in historical times seems to have been less favoured than whiskey and mead, a drink made from honey. By Arthur Guinness's time beer was not a particularly popular drink with the Irish, especially outside of the cities, and the local beers were noted for their sourness and poor quality.

The first beer that came from the Guinness brewery were simple ales, but around 1770 a new type of beer began to be imported from England. It contained roasted barley which gave it a distinctive dark colouring, and since it was extremely popular with the porters at London's Covent Gardens, was commonly known as 'Porter'. Guinness, along with other Irish brewers in Dublin and Cork, decided to try his hand at the new drink. Unlike the porters of most of his rivals his brew was an enduring success. By 1800 Guinness had switched over entirely to the production of porter and a phenomenal process of growth - which turned the St. James's Gate brewery into the largest on earth by 1900 - was already underway.

There are several varieties of Guinness

The Blue Loo pub, Glengarriff, Co. Cork.

O' Neill's and the Lighthouse pubs, Allihies, Co. Cork.

on sale in Ireland, but the most common is Guinness's Extra Stout, sold either on draught or in the familiar yellow labelled bottle. When the first metal containers for draught stout were introduced Dubliners nicknamed them iron lungs, which is why one sometimes hears calls for 'a pint of lung' from drinkers in the city's bars. A huge amount of Guinness is consumed in Ireland's pubs, as in the 1960's for example, when 80% of the beer drunk in Irish public houses was made by the company. With the strong mod-

ern trend towards lighter ales and lagers the predominate position of Guinness has diminished over the last decade, but its importance to Ireland's drinkers still cannot be overestimated. The pint of stout, drunk either from the old fashioned straight sided tumbler or the more modern handled tankard, remains by far the most common drink seen in the Irish pub.

There are many reasons for the ongoing popularity of Guinness, the most impor-

Cullen's pub, Rathdrum, Co. Wicklow.

tant needless to say being its uniquely rich taste. The lovers of Guinness span all social classes, from the poorest to the richest. The noted American millionaire and Art collector Chester Beatty, for instance, was in the habit of stating that the only reason he came to live in Ireland was for the Guinness. Even when dining with some of the worlds most famous statesmen and celebrities he would ask for a glass of stout in prefer-ence to the finest wines. Devotees of Joyce's ebon ale seem able to drink it by the gallon, not least the Welsh poet Dylan Thomas.....

'Don't call me morbid George Ring. I remember once I drank fourty-nine Guinnesses and I came home on the top of a bus. There's nothing morbid about a man who can do that. Right on top of the bus too, not just the upper deck .....''

Guinness, of course, is not the only stout brewed in Ireland. Cork, which also has a long history of brewing, offers two

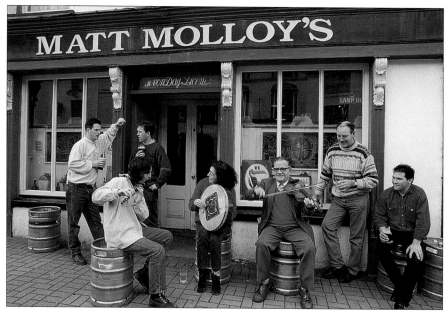

Matt Molloy's bar, Westport, Co. Mayo.

good stouts of its own, Murphy's and Beamish, to challenge the Dublin brand. The distinctive appearance of any pint of stout, whether Guinness or one of its rivals like Murphy's, has much to do with its worldwide appeal. There is something ritualistic in the way a good Irish barman will pour the drink from the tap, carefully filling and levelling it until the creamy white collar sits perfectly on the rich black stout, making the 'parish priest' as some wits describe the finished pint. Other good beers and stouts are brewed in Ireland, but as James Joyce reminds us, none can ever compare with the immortal stout made in Ireland by the Guinness family.

'For they garner the succulent berries of the hop and mass and sift and bruise and brew them and they mix therewith sour juices and bring the must to the sacred fire and cease not night and day from their toil, those cunning brothers, lords of the vat.'
(from Ulysses by James Joyce)

Durty Nelly's bar, Bunratty, Co. Clare.

Perhaps more than any other writer James Joyce reminds us of the important literary connections of the Irish pub, most famously in Dublin. In the city's egalitarian pubs it is not only poets who congregate, but also civil servants and dockers and factory workers. The term 'literary pub' sometimes seen in tour guides to the city is fallacious, since in any good pub members of every trade will be found. Even in the pubs associated with them, writers will be only one clique amongst many. Having said this, there is an unique lasting relationship between the city's poets, novelists and dramatists and her pubs, as the following quotes from three different poems about the city illustrate.

'A public house to half a hundred men
And the teacher, the solicitor and the bank clerk
In the hotel bar drinking for ten.'
(from 'Dublin Made Me' by Donagh MacDonagh,
in 'The Hungry Grass', Faber & Faber,

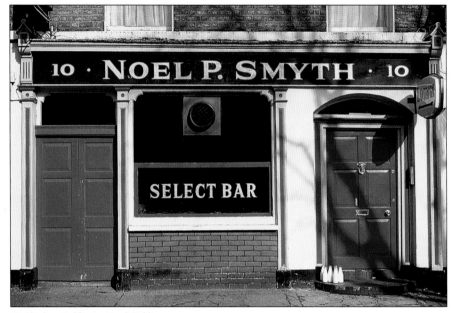

Smith's bar, Haddington Road, Dublin.

1947)

'And porter running from the taps
With a yellow head of cream'
(from 'Dublin' by Louis MacNeice)

'Go into a pub and listen well
If my voice still echoes there'
(from 'If Ever you Go To Dublin Town' by
Patrick Kavanagh
in Collected Poems, McGibbons & Kee,
1972)

The pubs of Dublin have an individual
flavour which owes much to their clientele. The average Dubliner has a character and way of talking uniquely his own,
whilst the everyday wit and repartee
amongst the population are famous.
The city's distinctive dialect has a turn of
phrase peculiar to itself and its store of
emotive slang words give conversation
overheard in Dublin pubs remarkable flu-
idity and richness. Brendan Behan must
be noted as the writer who, above all
others, was able to catch the Dublin

Portraits of the Dubliners' folk group, O Donaghue's pub, Dublin.

Pub signs, Dingle, Co. Kerry.

Kate Kearney's Cottage, Gap of Dunloe, Co. Kerry.

speech and use it for literary purposes. A great pubman himself, he was known in pubs all over the city but is most associated with McDaid's in Harry Street. The following excerpt from "The Big House" displays his mastery of the Dublin dialect. Two old women are discussing their dead soldier husbands.

(Granny Growl)   And me first husband was et be the Ashantees. All they found was a button and a bone.

(Granny Grunt)   Gods curse to the hungry bastards.

(Granny Growl)   But still an' all ma'm what business did he have going near them. Me second husband had more sense. He stopped in the militia and never went further than the Curragh for a fortnight.

(Granny Grunt)   Maria Concepta, do you remember when we used to wait for them coming off the train at Kingsbridge

Interior of Mulligan's bar, Poolebeg Street, Dublin.

and they after getting their bounty money and waiting on the station to be dismissed.

(Granny Growl) Deed and I do Teresa Avila and me provoked sergeant, he was an Englishman, would let a roar that'd go through you...

(Granny Grunt) That's the very way he used to shout. It used to thrill me through my boozem.

(from 'The Complete Plays of Brendan Behan,' Metheun 1960)

Inevitably, the pubs of Dublin feature predominately in the works of James Joyce. In the first decade of the 20th. century many of the pubs of Dublin were in their prime, and Joyce includes a number in his books. The Scotch House, now alas knocked down but once a famous landmark on Dublin's Quays, is the setting for the short story 'Counterparts' in 'Dubliners'. 'Ulysses'

Pub interior, Rostrevor, Co. Down.

has incidents and scenes in a number of pubs around the city centre. Most have changed utterly since 1904, or been demolished like Barney Kiernan's in Little Britain Street. Of all the pubs of Ulysses only Burke's of Poolbeg Street (now Mulligan's) has remained comparatively unchanged since Joyce's time. Today, just as in 1904, Mulligan's is a simple but attractive working man's pub.

If literature is thought of mainly in connection with the pubs of Dublin, Irish music is a heritage shared by pubs throughout Ireland. Traditional music cannot be learnt out of a book, it is a living music made by the people. Where else but a pub will the beginner begin to follow the advice of the noted Irish musicologist Breandán Breathnach.

'There is only one way of becoming a traditional player and singer, and that is by listening to genuine material performed in a traditional way.'

The roots of Irish traditional music are

The William Blake pub, Enniskillen, Co. Fermanagh.

probably very ancient and have their origins in the singing styles of prehistoric and Celtic Ireland. The earliest known instrument used in Ireland was the harp, depictions of which may be seen on early Christian stone crosses and shrines. How exactly the Irish harp was used in performance is not certain, but a picture in the 'Image of Irelande' drawn in the 16th. century suggests it was often played as background music to the verse and recitations of 'rhymers', or poets. Later, in the 17th. and 18th. centuries, the tunes of harpers like the famous Carolan formed the basis of what might be called a 'classical' Irish music. This tradition had almost died out by around 1800, when there was a renewal of interest in Irish music and Dublin craftsmen like John Egan began making beautiful concert and portable harps.

Although the Irish harp, carved with the figure of Hibernia, is the national symbol, it has not played a major part in the development of what we today call 'tra-

Traditional musicians , Milltown Malbay, Co. Clare.

Pub near Ballinrobe, Co. Mayo.

Dan Murphy's bar, Sneem, Co. Kerry.

ditional' music. This style probably began to take a recognizable Irish form in the 19th. century and has been evolving ever since. Its repertoire of tunes and songs come from a diverse variety of sources. Some are traditional or composed by known or unknown Irish musicians, whilst others might be versions of polkas, Music Hall songs or other material learnt from gramophone records. To a large extent what makes 'real' traditional music is not so much the piece as the way it played. It is not a formal or

composed music, but rather a wide range of personalised or improvised versions of tunes and songs played by individuals or groups within a shared musical culture.

On this level Irish traditonal music has a closer affinity with jazz, blues or bluegrass music rather than other folk or popular styles. Its growth and change depend upon personal interaction between its players and without this it stops being a living style and becomes

Wall sign, Co. Donegal.

Wall sign, Co. Wicklow.

sterile and formalised. There can be little doubt that the 'regional styles' of Irish fiddle playing developed through a few influential players in each area passing their music on to followers who established it in their locality. Even the great renewal of Irish traditional music following Sean O'Riada's ground breaking compositions and the Folk Boom of the 1960's, came about only because a comparatively small number of young musicians like Christy Moore and Donal

Lunney were prepared to learn their trade from older masters of the style.

The great contribution of the pub to the survival of Irish traditional music has been as a melting pot, where players can come together and learn from each other. Where it has become a mini- (or sometimes not so mini -) concert hall in which groups merely play set pieces to audiences, the pub has lost the spark that it gave to the tradition and become

Grindel's pub, Ballyhooly, Co. Cork.

a glorified cabaret. This is not written from a desire to condemn performances of Irish music in pubs and elsewhere, but to make the point that its essential driving force is that musicians sit down together to listen to each other and learn. Irish pubs, particularly those in western counties like Clare, have provided a congenial workshop in which this process may take place.

Theoretically Irish traditional music could be on a large number of conventional musical instruments. In fact the range of instruments used is quite narrow and for those unfamiliar with the subject, it might be as well to mention the most common. Apart from stringed instruments like the ubiquitous guitar, mandolin and banjo, introduced this century through the influence of American country and popular music, most owe something of their popularity or modern form to the drawing-rooms of Anglo-Irish landlords. Musical ability was valued by the aristocratic and middle classes of Georgian and Victorian

Hough's pub, Banagher, Co. Offaly.

Ireland and many instruments associated with traditional Irish music were introduced into Ireland through this channel.

Uillean (elbow) or Union pipes were first developed around 1700 from the traditional Irish and Scottish war pipes, but the modern version, which allows for the playing of non Irish music, probably evolved around 1800 for amateur and stage musicians. Today's uillean pipes are usually based on those made for the American market by the Taylor Bros. of Philledlphia in the second half of the 19th. century. Flutes - and later the cheaper tin whistle - also seem to have come into Ireland through main stream classical music and been adapted for traditional styles.

The most important single instrument of Irish music is probably the fiddle, which is simply a violin with metal strings. Its use as an accompaniment for dancing hints that it was the paramount instrument of the common people, played in every shebeen and grog house in the era before pubs. In earlier times the fiddle was played in a variety of local styles, which may still be heard in some small pubs. In the 1920's and 30's, however, the influence of recordings made in America by a Sligo man, Michael Coleman, led to what might be called a standard style of Irish fiddle playing. Another Irish-American, Francis O'Neill of the Chicago police, was the major single influence on the repertoire of Irish traditional music. The huge collection of melodies in his book, 'Music of Ireland', published in 1903, is the major single source of traditional tunes.

Other instruments have a less auspicious history than the fiddle. The one-sided goat skin bodhran drum is basically a simple tambourine, used by 'wren boys' and 'mummers' in Old Ireland but only introduced into traditional music by Sean O'Riada in modern times. Since it is so easy to play the bodhran has become the most common and most misused of all traditional instruments. The accordion ('an instrument in harmony with the sentiments of an assassin' as the American writer Ambrose Pierce wrote) and to a lesser extent the concertinas, are again comparatively recent introdutions to traditional music, but through the medium of the Ceili band have become well established.

These are the instruments of traditional Irish music, which can be heard any night of the week at hundreds of Irish

Pub interior, Allihies, Co. Cork.

The Temple bar, Dublin.

pubs. To the neophyte a pub 'session' might seem unstructered and haphazard, with some musicians not joining in some songs and long intervals between bursts of music. In fact there is a logical and long established etiquette for players and audience alike. Since no two musicians have exacly the same repertoire, common ground must be established for versions of songs or tunes. Sometimes a musician will not want to play, preferring to watch those who do to learn a new technique or styl-

istic variant. The audience are not at a concert watching a set preformance, they are witnessing the creative process at work in a series of near improvisations on often familiar tunes.

The little yelps, whoops and comments from spectators who know their music are not as random as they seem and mark key points in tunes or particularly fine passages of playing. Unlike a concert, the spectator is not there to participate or encourage the performance. The

The Matchmakers bar, Lisdoonvarna, Co. Clare.

best way for the onlooker to show his appreciation for the musicians is to simply buy them a round of drinks, not by approaching them individually but through the barman. Nor is it advisable to get to close or sit amongst the musicians, or for that matter record or photograph them without asking them first. The visitor who follows these simple rules is assured of a good night's entertainment and a chance of hearing some of the finest live music he has ever heard.

In the history of the Irish pub, traditional music must take the paramount position. However, musicians from other disciplines have been nurtured in Ireland's pubs and gone on to achieve local or world fame. In the 1960's white Rhythm and Blues could be heard in the smoky bars of many Dublin and Belfast pubs, performed by artist like Van Morrison, Rory Gallagher and Phil Lynnott. The punk movement of the late 1970's gave birth to notable bands like The Undertones and The Boomtown Rats,

Mc Swiggan's bar, Galway.

Dublin horse enjoying a pint of plain.

whilst in the 1980's the young U2 and Sinead O'Connor cut their musical teeth in similiar venues. Even today, minority taste musical styles like Bluegrass, Cajun and Jazz find an audience mainly in the lounges of bars and pubs. The profit from the sale of alcohol allows the pub to sustain and expand musical tastes with a freedom that more formal clubs or concert halls could not afford. Today, piped music and the Karaoke machine are beginning to dominate the public house, and young and well established performers alike are finding it harder to get venues. This is a great tragedy, since without the support of the pub the great and varied stream of music which has so enriched Irish culture is liable to dry up.

Byrne's pub, Grenane, Co. Wicklow.

Morrissey's bar, Abbeyleix, Co. Laois.

Bushe's bar, Baltimore, West Cork.

Books in this series:

The Irish Pub
The Irish Cottage
The Irish Castle & Abbey
Ireland

Liam Blake was born in Dublin, he is the author of several photographic books and has exhibited his photographs in solo and group exhibitions. He has won many awards including best photographic book 1985.

David Pritchard was educated at Trinity College, Dublin and now lives in South Wicklow. His published works include books on Irish postage stamps, an illustrated anthology of Irish poetry and a number of books for Real Ireland Design.